WOMEN ON FIRE

CARRIERS OF THE FIRE, VOL.3

FRANK "JJ" DI PIETRO

Women on Fire (Carriers of the Fire: Vol.3)

Copyright © 2021 by Christos Publishing

P.O. Box 1333, Lee's Summit, Missouri 64063

All rights reserved. Printed in the United States of America.

ISBN: 978-1-950053-22-3

Layout by Rachel Greene for elfinpen designs

TABLE OF CONTENTS

FOREWORD

God has used many women in helping to prepare the way to establish His revival movements from generation to generation. In this book, Frank Di Pietro vividly portrays the calling and ministries of many of these dynamic, God-called ladies.

My husband, Pastor Steve Gray, and I have been graced by God to be voices of global revival to our generation, since leading the historic Smithton Outpouring in 1996 to 2000. Our congregation, World Revival Church, led the way in the Kansas City Revival seen weekly on Daystar Christian Television Network from 2008 to 2011; and we continue to maintain the spirit of revival to this day, as we anticipate another global outpouring of unprecedented proportions. God will certainly need an army of His daughters ready to participate in that.

I have observed in Frank that although he is an avid scholar of the history of revival, he does not live in the past and dream of a better tomorrow. He is a participant now, vigorously contending for the revival of God's presence and power for his generation.

The reader will appreciate Frank's in-depth presentation of women who were pioneers in the faith. You will be inspired and encouraged as you read of their faith, commitment, and sacrifice to birth and maintain revival.

— Kathy Gray
Founding Pastor of World Revival Church
of Kansas City

"Awake, awake, Deborah! Awake, awake…"

(JUDGES 5:12)

CHAPTER ONE

FANNY J. CROSBY

"Whether we think of or speak to God; whether we act or suffer for Him; all is prayer when we have no other object than His love, and the desire of pleasing Him."

— JOHN WESLEY

"I would rather teach one man to pray than ten to preach."

— CHARLES SPURGEON

"It is not our business to make the message acceptable, but to make it available. We are not to see that they like it, but that they get it."

— DR. VANCE HAVNER

A Hymn: "To God Be the Glory"…
"To God be the glory, great things He has done;

So loved He the world that He gave us His Son,

Who yielded His life an atonement for sin,

And opened the life gate that all may go in.

Praise the Lord, praise the Lord,

Let the earth hear His voice!

Praise the Lord, praise the Lord,

Let the people rejoice!

O come to the Father, through Jesus the Son,

And give Him the glory,

Great things He has done."

— FANNY J. CROSBY

Fanny Crosby's legacy lives on through her many songs—8,000 according to her own recollection. Many of her hymns still, after almost a century, are remembered and sung weekly in services around the world. They shook the spirits of thousands of worshipers in great evangelistic meetings of such men as D. L. Moody and Billy Graham and were even intermingled with the awesome worship music that came out of the last three revivals (Toronto Blessing, Brownsville Revival, The Smithton Outpouring). In all her songs there is an innocence and intimacy that pulls you deeper into communion with the Lord during worship. Two hymns, "Safe in the Arms of Jesus" and "Saved by Grace," have been documented with thousands of conversions on hearing them the very first time. Not all her songs survive today; many have passed into oblivion, but when you write as many hymns as she did, publishers would be hesitant to print a hymnal with one author. So Woodman Bradbury supplies us with the answer to that problem:

"She [Fanny] recognized the fact that so large an output would lower the value of her name; and her eight thousand hymns have appeared under a hundred or so different pseudonyms! If the reader comes across the names of Rose Atherton, Florence Booth, Ella Dale, Frances Hope, Ruth Harmon, Victoria Frances, let him pay mental homage to Fanny Crosby; and he will be surprised to learn that the same homage is due when he sees the names of James Apple, James Black, Rian J. Sterling, W. Robert Lindsay, and others... The theology of her hymns is uniformly Evangelical. The author believes humanity to be sinful and in need of salvation; and she magnifies the love of God,

the grace of Christ and the power of the Holy Spirit... Her songs form an appropriate atmosphere for evangelistic preaching: they produce conviction of sin and conversion."

In her own words Fanny calls herself "a worshiping soul" and her hymns are "the incense." Fanny's talent was an inspiration from God. She never wrote out her hymns but totally completed each one in her mind and then dictated it to a secretary. It is said that she could thus compose a dozen or more hymns and carry them around in her head days at a time before finally committing them to paper complete with verse and music. With as many as two hundred different pen names, over one million copies of her music were printed. An amazing feat for someone but especially for her; Fanny Crosby was blind. Blind all of her life. Is it any wonder that Fanny Crosby, the greatest hymn writer in the history of the Christian Church, would one day write in song, *"And I shall see Him face to face, and tell the story—saved by grace."*

Frances Jane "Fanny" Crosby was born in a town called Southeast, Putnam County, New York, on March 24, 1820. She would never remember her father who died before she was a year old. Her mother lived to be 91. When Fanny was six weeks old, she caught a slight cold in her eyes. The regular family physician was out of town so her father asked another country doctor to treat her. He prescribed hot mustard poultices to be applied to her eyes, which destroyed her sight completely! An outcry arose against the ill-educated doctor and before he could be prosecuted he fled town, never to be heard of again. Fanny, always noted for her happy and cheerful disposition, never harbored any resentment for the doctor but believed it was the plan of the Lord for her life. When she was in her eighties she recalled her feelings for the poor doctor:

> "...I have not, for a moment, in more than eighty-five years, felt a spark of resentment against him; for I always believed that the good Lord, in His infinite mercy, by this means consecrated me to the work that I am still permitted to do. When I remember how I have been blessed, how can I complain? Blindness cannot keep the sunlight of hope from the trustful soul. One of the easiest resolves that I formed in my... heart was to leave all care to

yesterday, and to believe that the morning would bring forth its own peculiar joy."

One day a preacher sadly remarked, *"I think it is a great pity that the Master did not give you sight when he showered so many other gifts upon you."*

Fanny quickly replied, *"Do you know that if at birth I had been able to make one petition, it would have been that I should be born blind?"*

"Why?" asked the surprised minister.

"Because when I get to heaven, the first face that shall ever gladden my sight will be that of my savior!"

When Fanny was five years old, neighbors and friends raised money to send her to the best eye specialist in the country, Dr. Valentine Mott. After an examination the doctor sadly said, *"Poor child, I am afraid you will never see again."* While her mother took the news with sorrow, it never once bothered young Fanny. At the age of eight she wrote her first recorded poetry:

"O what a happy soul I am! Although I cannot see, I am resolved that in this world, contented I

will be. How many blessings I enjoy, that other people don't. To weep and sigh because I'm blind, I CANNOT AND I WON'T!"

While her mother was busy making a living for the family, Fanny was influenced most by her grandmother, who spent many hours describing the things of nature and heaven to her. At night her grandmother would call Fanny to her rocking chair and the two would kneel in prayer together for hours. Fanny, through her grandmother, acquired a thorough knowledge of the Bible, studying and learning by heart four or five chapters a week. Before long she could repeat from memory the first four books of the Old Testament, Ruth, most of the Psalms, the Book of Proverbs, Song of Solomon, and the four Gospels. It was through this knowledge of the Scriptures that she would develop the themes and inspiration of her many hymns.

At the age of 15 one of Fanny's dreams came true; she was admitted to the New York Institute for the Blind. So on March 3, 1835, she left for New York City and stayed at the school for the next 23 years, 12 years as a student and 11 as a teacher.

From her early childhood Fanny had felt the urge to write poetry, now here, at the institution, her abilities began to assert themselves with renewed force. She received little encouragement from her teachers but visitors gave her all she needed. The school was world famous and the upper crust of society was always touring the school. The famous poet William Cullen Bryant visited the school one day and gave Fanny much encouragement, after chancing to read some of her verses. She said afterwards, *"He never knew how much he did for me by those few words."* Then one day, Dr. Combe of Boston came to examine the heads of the blind students. As he felt Fanny's head, he exclaimed, *"And here is a poetess. Give her every possible encouragement. Read the best books to her and teach her the finest that is in poetry. You will hear from this young lady some day."* This was the pat on the back that she needed. Poetry began to flow from her heart and mind in abundance. It wasn't long before her work was becoming well-known.

An unpleasant episode of her life happened about this time. There was a cholera outbreak in New York City. The epidemic spread throughout the city, and the cry of "bring out your dead" could be heard nightly. Many of the blind caught the infection and died. Fanny herself had the initial symptoms one afternoon. Bravely she kept the news to herself, took the medicine, practiced the precautions, and committed herself to God in prayer. When she woke the next morning, she was perfectly well.

In the autumn of 1843, she was a representative of the Institute before the Congress of the United States in hopes of receiving an appropriation to continue its work. Fanny, although blind, said she could feel the stern stares of these men of politics as she took the podium. She paid tribute to Congress in an original verse she wrote, then began paying tribute to the Lord. Words such as these had never before been spoken within these walls of this "Hall of Meeting." As one visitor recalls:

> *"She delivered no stirring oration, nor pathetic story but simply recited her original poems about the tender care of a loving Savior. She spoke with conviction, as though she had seen the Savior face to face."*

Those present at the notable assembly that day were names that are forever etched in American history such as; John Quincy Adams, Thomas E. Benton,

Hamilton Fish, Henry A. Wise, Alexander Stevens, Jefferson Davis, and Nathan Toombs. As Fanny spoke a silence fell upon the attendees and the presence of the Lord filled the room. Before long sobs could be heard coming from these renowned men and tears were glistening on their cheeks as her message brought a healing to many of their souls. Of course, the appropriation was obtained.

Fanny was thrust into the limelight almost overnight. Throughout her life she made friends with many of the great political and religious leaders of her time and every one of them remarked that once you met her you could not forget her. President Martin Van Buren dined with her many times and remained one of her closest friends. She would always talk about the virtues of another friend, President William Henry Harrison; unfortunately he served but one month. When President Tyler came to visit the Institute, Fanny welcomed him with an original poem. Her friendship with President Polk was close and inspiring. She also enjoyed a close friendship with President Cleveland for more than half a century, for at one time he was the secretary of the Institute while she was teaching there. She had a close friendship with the great statesman Henry Clay and numerous times they could be seen weeping together as she shared with him those special intimate moments she had with her Savior.

Of course, her closest and dearest friend was that of Jesus. Even though her life revolved around the Lord, she always felt something was lacking in her walk. It was a complete conversion, a sanctification, with her Lord that she lacked, and in 1851, at the age of 31, the Holy Spirit suddenly poured into her life. This *"glorious happening"* occurred at a revival service held at the John Street Methodist Church in New York. Recalling the incident years later, she said:

> *"Some of us went every evening, but although I sought peace, I could not find the joy I craved, until one evening I arose and went forward alone. After the prayer the congregation began to sing that grand old consecration hymn, 'Alas, and did my Savior bleed?' And when they reached the third line of the fifth stanza, 'here Lord, I give myself away,' I surrendered myself to the Savior, and my very soul was flooded with celestial light. I sprang to my feet, shouting 'Hallelujah!'"*

In 1858 Fanny married Alexander Van Alstyne, also a blind teacher at the Institute. The marriage was a happy one and lasted 44 years until Alexander's death in 1902. The couple had one child who died while still a baby. It wasn't long after the death of their child that Fanny wrote one of her most famous hymns, *"Safe in the Arms of Jesus,"* which was to become a comfort to thousands.

"Pass Me Not" was her first hymn to win worldwide attention. Fanny composed this in 1868 after a prison service. As she spoke to the prisoners one of them cried out, *"O Lord, don't pass me by!"* She was so moved that she went home and wrote her famous plea. Ira Sankey said, *"No hymn was more popular at the meetings in London in 1875 than this one."* One hard drinking Englishman heard the crowd singing it and whispered to himself, *"Oh, I wish He would not pass me by."* The next night the service began with the same hymn and he was saved. He began carrying a copy of the hymn with him every day, and 40 years later, as a successful businessman in America, he met Fanny and ran to her and hugged her until her eyes were about to pop.

Even though Fanny rubbed elbows with some of the most prominent men of her time, the two men she considered the greatest were the preacher and the song-man... the evangelistic duo of Moody and Sankey. D. L. Moody and Ira D. Sankey traveled the world together bringing the gospel to thousands. Moody did the preaching and Sankey did the singing. Fanny writes:

> *"In the thought of Christian people everywhere throughout the world the names, Moody and Sankey, are linked together; and I have been not a little honored in having these great evangelists among my dearest friends... So strong was the friendship existing between Mr. Moody and Mr. Sankey that we used to call them 'David and Jonathan'; and I am sure that the modern church has not known two men more devoted to the work of Christian evangelism; and so they went far and near, telling the old, old story in sermon and in gospel song, until the influence of their meetings spread through all classes of society."*

Fanny remembers a time during the revival Moody and Sankey held in Northfield, Illinois, during the summer of 1894:

"My own recollections of Northfield bring back many incidents... While Mr. Moody was holding a series of evangelistic services in England, I helped with the services here at home. One evening Mr. Sankey came to me and said, 'Will you say something tonight? There is a request from the audience that you speak.' I felt I was not prepared for the occasion and so I said, 'Oh, Mr. Sankey, I cannot speak before such an array of talent.' 'Fanny, do you speak to please man or to please God?' Sankey said. 'Why I hope to please God,' I replied. 'Well then,' he said, 'Go out and do your duty.' During my remarks that evening I repeated for the first time in public the words to 'Saved by Grace,' although the hymn had been written by me more than two years before that summer, but it had never been published or used in any way. 'Where have you kept that piece?' asked Mr. Sankey, when I returned to my seat. I told him that I had kept it stored away for an emergency. There was a reporter present that evening; he copied the hymn as I gave it; and a few weeks later it appeared in a religious paper... and

thus the hymn was sent forth on its mission to the world."

"Some day the silver cord will break,
And I no more as now shall sing;
But oh, the joy when I shall wake
Within the palace of the King!
And I shall see Him face to face,
And tell the story—Saved by grace.
And I shall see Him face to face,
And tell the story—Saved by grace."

Fanny writes after the death of Moody:

"Dwight Lyman Moody was a wonderful man; and he did his own work in a unique way, which was sometimes no less daring than original. The following passage from the Holy Book is in my mind as I think of his blameless life: 'Blessed are the dead which die in the Lord from henceforth. Yea, saith the Spirit, that they may rest from their labors, and their works do follow them.'

"It is a blessed joy that his companion, Mr. Sankey, has been spared to the present hour; and

that during the last twenty-five years he has been a close associate of mine in writing gospel hymns… The friendship of this talented man is one of my priceless jewels."

Another interesting incident in Fanny's walk with God makes one chuckle:

"Among the great number of hymns that I have written, eight thousand perhaps, it is not always possible for me to remember even the best of them. For this reason I have made laughable mistakes. One morning, for example, at the Northfield revival the audience sang 'Hide Me, O My Savior.' But I did not recognize this hymn as my own production; and therefore I may be pardoned for saying that I was much pleased with it. Turning to Mr. Sankey, I asked, 'Where did you get that piece?' He paid no particular attention to my question, for he supposed I was merely joking… it was again used at the afternoon service; and then I was determined to know who wrote it. 'Mr. Sankey,' I said. 'Now you must tell me who is the author of 'Hide Me, O My Savior." '

Really,' he replied, 'don't you recall who wrote that hymn? You ought to remember, for you are the guilty one.'"

Fanny's hymns were popular worldwide. Soldiers in battle would use the titles of her hymns or their stated number in hymnals as passwords. When Bishop James Hannington was brutally murdered by savages in Uganda, Africa, his diary was recovered. In it, he tells of being dragged away to be murdered while singing "Safe in the Arms of Jesus." Another story was during World War I in 1918. A Finnish engineer tells of capturing a town and taking a number of prisoners. Seven of them were to be shot at dawn the next day. One of the doomed men began to sing, "Safe in the Arms of Jesus"… One after another his comrades fell to their knees and began to sing. They asked to be allowed to die with their faces uncovered. Then with hands raised to heaven, they sang this song as the execution shots rang out. The Officer in charge met Christ himself that very hour as a result of that witness.

"Safe in the Arms of Jesus" was one of the first American Gospel hymns to be transcribed into foreign languages. Mr. Ira Sankey remembers:

"Once when preaching in London, I went to Basel, Switzerland, for a few days' rest. The evening I got there I heard under my window the most beautiful volume of song. I looked out and saw about fifty people who were singing "Safe in the Arms of Jesus" in their own language. I recognized the tune and spoke to them through an interpreter. The next evening, rest was forgotten, and I held a song service in an old French church in that city. The church was packed with people and many stood outside on the street."

The hymn we started out this story with, *"To God Be the Glory" (ED NOTE:* It has always been one of my favorite hymns), was written in 1873. Sankey published it in his first hymnbook in 1873 but it was not found in later editions. It was rediscovered in 1954 and it was sung by George Beverly Shea and the Billy Graham Crusade Choir in Toronto in 1955. Since then, it has become one of Fanny's most beloved hymns.

Ira Sankey did more than any other single individual to popularize Fanny's songs. The thousands upon thousands that flocked to the Moody-Sankey revivals sang her songs until they became a heritage of that generation.

Fanny wrote hymns up to her last day. Her latter days were spent in Bridgeport, Connecticut, with an old friend, Mrs. Booth. On her last night she dictated a letter of comfort to a sorrowing friend, whose daughter had recently died. At three o'clock the next morning, Mrs. Booth, going to wake Fanny for prayer, found her unconscious. And so Fanny died "Safe in the Arms of Jesus," just short of her 95th birthday. Her funeral filled the church and her minister, George M. Brown, closed the services with this statement:

> *"There must have been a royal welcome when this queen of sacred song burst the bonds of death and passed into the glories of heaven."*

A royal welcome indeed. I am sure that celebration will be noted in the annals of eternity as Fanny stood before her Lord and Savior, with her eyes wide open staring in wonderment at His face. And not being able to withhold her excitement burst into song with the choirs of angels all singing her own favorite and most popular hymn of adoration:

"Blessed assurance, Jesus is mine!
Oh, what a foretaste of glory divine!
Heir of salvation, purchase of God,
Born of his Spirit, washed in His blood.
This is my story, this is my song,
Praising my Savior all the day long;
This is my story, this is my song,
Praising my Savior all the day long."

"Make a joyful shout to the Lord, all you lands!
Serve the Lord with gladness; come before His
presence with singing."

(PSALM 100:1-2)

CHAPTER TWO

HATTIE MAE WIATT

"Let the little children come to me, and do not forbid them; for such is the kingdom of heaven."

— JESUS OF NAZARETH

"Even a child is known by his deeds, by whether what he does is pure and right."

— KING SOLOMON
(PROVERBS 20:11)

"Whoever receives one of these little children in My name receives Me; and whoever receives Me, receives not Me but Him who sent Me."

— YESHUA (YAHWEH IS SALVATION)

It was 1884, and the city of Philadelphia was in the grip of one of the coldest winters in memory. But on this particular Sunday, the temperature had warmed a bit and was in the low forties, a biting wind blew around the corner of Berks and Mervine Streets where the Grace Baptist Church was located. It was a very small church in an area where, as one man put it, *"The industrious, honorable, upright and saving classes of society lived, not the wealthy and great."* The church being so small, was always crowded, tickets of admission to services were obtained, sometimes weeks in advance for every service. The Sunday school classroom, used as an overflow room, was also crowded with the rest of the congregation.

Little Hattie Mae Wiatt lived in a small ramshackle tenement building near the church. For weeks, she listened as her friends talked about meeting with Jesus every week at Sunday school. Hattie made up her mind that she would meet Him, too. Her mother dressed Hattie as best she could and sent her off with her friends to the Sunday school annex. Hattie was 6 years old at the time. Can you imagine sending a child off like that in today's society? Hattie arrived early and was told to wait outside until the "regular" children had all arrived. She watched as child after child was let inside. The teacher then stuck her head out and said there was no more room and promptly closed the door.

Shortly, the Pastor of the church was on his way to teach the adult Sabbath School, when he noticed a sobbing little girl standing by the entrance gate. He looked down at the small face streaked with tears and the crusty little nose caked from the cold and asked her why she was crying. *"I cannot go to meet Jesus in Sunday school,"* she said. *"They have no room because it is too crowded."* He knew there was always room for such small children, but then seeing her shabby, unkempt appearance, he realized the true reason she was not admitted.

This godly man then relates:

> *"I took her up in my arms, lifted her to my shoulders and then as she held onto my head—an embrace I could never forget—I carried her through the crowd in the hall, into the Sunday school room and seated her in a chair away back in a dark corner."*

As he carried Hattie into the room, his stern gaze met that of the teacher. Tears immediately filled the woman's eyes as the Holy Ghost's conviction fell upon her. If Jesus' presence was not in the room before, it was now.

Hattie was so happy they found room for her; she went to bed that night asking Jesus for a bigger place, so that all children could come and worship Him. She then decided to start saving whatever she could to help build a larger church.

Hattie and the pastor became good friends. Over the next two years, he met with Hattie at her home, and the Gospel was spread not only to Hattie's parents but also to other families in that building. Hattie shared her friend Jesus with anybody that would listen and brought a touch of salvation to many others in and around her neighborhood. Whenever she and the pastor were together Hattie would ask him to *"pray to Jesus to help build our little church bigger, so more children can come to Sunday school."*

"One morning," the pastor tells us, *"I came down to the church from my home and as I came by Hattie's house, she was going up the street to school."* (Hattie was 8 years old at the time) *"As we met I said, 'Hattie, we're going to have a larger Sunday school room'* and *she said, 'I hope you will. It is always so crowded.' 'Well,' I replied, 'when we get the money with which to erect a school building, we are going to construct one large enough to get all the little*

children in and we are going to begin very soon to raise the money for it.'" Years later, he told his congregation that the future Sunday school room was just an imaginary vision but he had wished to make conversation with the child.

A few days later, he had heard that Hattie was very sick (she had contracted diphtheria). *"Her family asked me to come and see the child and pray for her, which I did. I left and walked up the street, praying for the little girl's recovery and yet, all the time, with the conviction that it was not to be."* The next day, Hattie was dead. Her parents called for the kind-hearted pastor, who had befriended their daughter, to handle the funeral arrangements. He tells us:

> *"...As her poor little body was being moved, a worn and crumpled red purse was found, which seemed to have been rummaged from some trash dump. Inside was found 57 cents and a note scribbled in childish handwriting, which read: 'This is to help build the little church bigger, so more children can go to Sunday school.' For two years she had saved for this offering of love."*

When the Pastor tearfully read that note, he knew instantly what he would do. Carrying this note and the cracked, red pocketbook to the pulpit, he told the story of her unselfish love and devotion. He challenged his deacons to get busy and raise enough money for a larger building. But the story does not end there.

A newspaper reporter happened to be at the church that Sunday morning and wrote all about what was said and subsequently published it. Newspapers around the country picked up the story from the national wire. A wealthy realtor who read this story sent word and offered to sell the church a parcel of land worth over $30,000 dollars. When he was told that the church could not pay that much, he offered to sell it to them for a lot less in payments and a down payment of 57 cents. Church members got excited and made larger donations. Checks and money came from far and wide. Within five years, God increased little Hattie's gift to $250,000 dollars, a high sum for that time in turn of the century dollars. Her unselfish love had paid large dividends. That's called "Kingdom" economy.

To make a long story short, when and if you are in the city of Philadelphia, look up that church. It is now called Temple Baptist Church, with a seating capacity of 3,500. You'll also want to see an extension of the church, Temple University, higher education for law, medicine, dentistry and of course, theology. Hundreds graduate yearly into the ministry of various denominations since it is a non-denominational institution. Thousands upon thousands are now preaching the Gospel worldwide because of Hattie's 57 cents.

There is also the Good Samaritan hospital now called Temple University Hospital, founded and supported by the money from this church. It was a hospital that was founded to minister and help the poor and destitute. Also, walk through the huge Sunday school building that houses hundreds of beautiful children, bused in from all around the city, built so that no child in the area will ever need to be left outside during Sunday school again.

In one of the rooms in the old church may be seen the picture of the sweet face of the little girl Hattie Mae Wiatt, whose 57 cents, so sacrificially saved, made such a remarkable impact in the Kingdom of God. Alongside her picture is a portrait of her kind Pastor, Dr. Russell H. Conwell, who later authored a book that became a best-seller for over a century, *Acres of Diamonds.*

"... *Therefore, whoever humbles himself as this little child is the greatest in the Kingdom of Heaven.*"

(MATTHEW 18:4)

CHAPTER THREE
PANDITA RAMABAI

"Where is the hope of revival
God's Holy Spirit outpoured
Convicting of sin, and of judgment,
and righteousness of the Lord?
The lost ones will yield to God's Spirit
when Christians, cleansed, weep and pray;
God's Living Water flows outward;
This is 'Revival—God's Way!'"

— ESTELLE GIFFORD JACKSON

"I do not understand Christian people who are
not thrilled by the whole idea of revival... If
you want a perfect exposition of 1 Corinthians
1:25-31, read books on revival."

— DAVID MARTYN LLOYD-JONES

"I was born to fight devils and factions. It is my business to remove obstructions, to cut down thorns, to fill up quagmires, and to open and make straight paths. But if I may have some failing let me rather speak the truth with too great severity than once to act the hypocrite and conceal the truth."

— MARTIN LUTHER

"Before Thine ever blazing Throne, We have no luster of our own."

— OLIVER WENDELL HOLMES

In 1989, the Government of India issued a commemorative stamp of Pandita Ramabai and later named her "Woman of the Millennium." The following is taken from the official brochure of the stamp from the Department of Post, India:

"Pandita Ramadai, the youngest daughter of Anant Shastri, was a social reformer, a champion for the emancipation of women in India, a pioneer in education. Left totally alone

by the time she was 23, Ramabai acquired a great reputation as a Sanskrit [Hindu] scholar before meeting the Lord Jesus Christ as her personal Savior and Lord."

We Americans usually think of India as a country that is over-populated, disease-ridden, and poverty-stricken. It is a country that has entirely too many cows. We American Christians look at India as a country that is totally pagan in its beliefs and controlled by the Hindu priests. Both views are far from the truth. India is one of the most prosperous up-and-coming nations in today's world. On the Spiritual side, we in our American go-to-church-once-a-week-and-pay-our-tithes-and-sing-in-the-choir Christianity need to hear what a Christian leader in India named Bakht Singh has to say about us:

"The indigenous churches in India have a great burden for America just now... and are praying that God will visit your country with revival... You feel sorry for us in India because of our poverty in material things. We who know the Lord in India feel sorry for you in America

*because of your spiritual poverty. We pray that
God may give you gold tried in the fire which
He has promised to those who know the power
of His resurrection... In our churches we spend
four or five or six hours in prayer and worship,
and frequently our people wait on the Lord in
prayer all night; but in America after you have
been in church for one hour, you begin to look at
your watches. We pray that God may open your
eyes to the true meaning of worship... To
attract people to meetings, you have great
dependence on posters, on advertising, on
promotion, and on the build-up of a human
being. In India we have nothing more than the
Lord Himself and we find that He is sufficient.
Before a Christian meeting in India we never
announce who the speaker will be. When the
people come, they come to seek the Lord and not
a human being. We have had as many as
12,000 people come together just to worship the
Lord... We are praying that the people in
America might also come to church with a
hunger for God and not merely a hunger to see
some form of amusement or hear choirs or the
voice of a favorite man."*

Born in Karnataka in 1858, Ramabai was destined to be a woman of change in a time when the "status quo" was all there was to be. She was a champion of women's rights, a poet, and a scholar. Born and raised a Hindu, later becoming a Christian, she would not tie herself to the restriction of the denominations but would carve her own spiritual path to a personal relationship with the one true God. In the process she would draw criticism from Hindus and Christians alike. Through it all she would be acclaimed as a *"mother of modern India."*

Her father, Anant Dongre, a wealthy Hindu Guru, scandalized his high caste friends by teaching his wife and later his daughters to read the Sanskrit classics (ancient Hindu scriptures). In 1880, Ramabai would write about the Hindu attitudes toward women that she faced as a young woman: *"Women were considered to have no minds. They are lower than pigs."* The status of women was not much above cattle. The practice among the Hindu higher castes was to betroth young girls to much older men. Ramabai's own father at the time of his marriage was over forty and her mother nine. Her father had been astonished to overhear an Indian princess recite verses in the Sanskrit language. He made up his mind that when he married, he would teach his wife to read the ancient Hindu scriptures. This was so against the normal treatment of women that he had to move his wife into the Gungamul forest of Southern India, away from the prying eyes of his friends and the priests. Ramabai was born in that forest, and when she was eight years old her mother began teaching her Sanskrit. She learned many of the languages of India: Marathi, Bengali, Hindustani, Kanarese, and English. By the time she was twenty, she could recite 18,000 verses of the Puranas, a Hindu holy book.

Ramabai's father, although regarded as wise and holy, had an emptiness in him that he could not understand. A hunger that could not be filled with the Hindu scriptures left him very unhappy with his spiritual life. Not understanding the urging of the Holy Spirit and trying to seek peace, he led his family on futile pilgrimages seeking what he called the "unknown God." Later, Ramabai would write about those days:

> *"We had no common sense and foolishly spent all the money we had in hand in giving alms... to please the gods... We went to several sacred places and temples, to worship different gods*

and to bathe in sacred rivers and tanks to free ourselves from sin and curse, which brought poverty upon us. We prostrated ourselves before the stone and metal images of the gods and prayed before them day and night... but nothing came of all this futile effort to please the gods... The stone images remained as hard as ever and never answered our prayers."

During this time a severe famine spread through India, and with all their money gone to the priests, Ramadai's family went days without food. In her own words, Ramadai elaborates on the day her father, dying of starvation, called her to his side:

"Though his blind eyes could see me no longer, he held me tightly in his arms, and stroking my head and cheeks, he told me, in a few words broken by emotion, to remember how he loved me, how he had taught me to do right and never depart from the way of righteousness. His last loving command to me was to lead an honorable life... and to serve God all my life. He did not know the one and only true God, but served the ... unknown God with all his heart and

> *strength; and was desirous that his children should serve Him to the last. 'Remember, my child,' he said, 'You are my youngest and most beloved child. I have given you into the hand of our God; you are His, and to Him alone you must belong, and serve Him all your life.'"*

Her father soon died and so did her mother and sister. With just her brother, Ramadai started a quest to find that spiritual truth her father was telling her about. They traveled 4,000 miles throughout India, suffering cold, hunger, and thirst, even at times burying their bodies in sand to keep warm. All for nothing. Finally giving up, they settled in Calcutta where the Hindu scholars, impressed by her immense knowledge, called her *"Pandita,"* which means "learned." It was in Calcutta that Ramabai first heard about Christ. Being raised under the Hindu teachings that rewards are earned by pilgrimages and payments to the priests, she discovered that true salvation, through the blood of Jesus Christ, is a free gift from God. The gospel of Christ was the purest expression of her own spiritual intuitions, especially her growing belief that to serve women and the poor was a religious and not just a social work. Robert Ellsberg writes about Ramabai:

"Her travels in India... sensitized her to the bleak plight of widows and orphans... Ramabai set out to do something about this social problem, establishing centers for widows and orphans in Poona and later Bombay... Soon Ramabai had become the leading advocate for the rights and welfare of women in India... In 1883, she accepted an invitation by a congregation of Anglican nuns to visit England... She undertook a serious study of the Bible and asked to be baptized."

Ramabai traveled to the United States where she spoke to assemblies about India's needs and treatment of women, saying, *"It is very well to be called 'Pandita,' but such honors need to be turned to good purposes."* The people were shocked to hear how low Indian women, especially widows, were treated. Some burned alive on their husband's funeral pyres. Many were forced to become slaves or sent to temples as prostitutes to make money for the priests. Ramabai wrote a book entitled *The High Caste Hindu Women.* An excerpt from the book follows:

> *"There are thousands of priests and men learned in sacred lore... They neglect and oppress the widows, and devour widows' houses... hire them out to wicked men so long as they can get money; and when the poor, miserable slaves are no longer pleasing to their cruel masters, they turn them out in the street to beg their livelihood, to suffer the horrible consequences of sin, to carry the burden of shame, and finally to die the death worse than that of a starved street dog. The so-called sacred places... those veritable hells on earth... have become the graveyards of countless widows and orphans."*

She married at the age of twenty-two, but her husband died of cholera after sixteen months. She was left with a daughter, whom she named *"Manorama,"* meaning "Hearts Joy."

While in America, she was interested in organizations formed that would support her in opening schools for women and girls. After several days of prayer, Ramabai opened a refuge for women called *"Mukti,"* which means "salvation" in many Indian languages. The Hindu priests' complained that she was betraying her own culture and convinced the women that to go to the refuge would be sure death. Ramabai elaborates more on this:

> *"…Many widows refused to come to Mukti. Their minds were filled with dread of Christians… They think that some day after they are well fattened they will be hung head downward, and a great fire will be built underneath, and oil will be extracted from them to be sold at a fabulously large price for medical purposes. Others think they will be put into mills and their bones ground… They cannot understand that anyone would be kind to them without some selfish purpose."*

She, therefore, promised not to pressure the Hindu girls into becoming Christians. But she did offer the Bible to them, should they desire to learn about it. Many, through reading the Bible and observing Ramabai's godly life, converted to Christianity. Women came from all over the country. *"Many were girl brides so abused they were terrified of a touch and even older women, snarling like animals from years of cruelty."* It wasn't long before Ramabai declared the school completely Christian.

Ramabai, through all this, felt that something in her spiritual walk was missing. She had heard of a newness and a closeness in walking with God she did not possess, a baptism in the Holy Spirit that still was not a reality to her yet. In December 1904, she heard about the Holy Ghost revival in Wales. News of the Welsh Revival was sweeping across the world, and the revival fire was now burning in India. Ramabai longed to see revival among the helpless women in India. So she started prayer circles of *"about ten girls each, urging them to pray for the salvation of all nominal Christians in India and across the world."* She relates later:

> *"I was brought to the conviction that mine was only an intellectual belief... a belief in which there was no life. It looked for salvation in the future after death, and consequently my soul had not 'passed from death unto life.' God showed me how very dangerous my position was, and what a wretched and lost sinner I was, and how necessary it was to obtain salvation in the present, and not in some future time. I repented long; I became very restless and almost ill and passed many sleepless nights. The Holy Spirit got hold of me that I could not rest until I found*

salvation then and there. So I prayed earnestly to pardon my sins for the sake of Jesus Christ and let me realize that I had really got salvation through Him. I believed God's promise and took Him at His word, and when I had done this, my burden rolled away, and I realized that I was forgiven and freed from the power of sin."

At first there were seventy women in her prayer circles, with more and more women being added daily. Each circle was given the names of ten unsaved girls and women to pray for. Within six months there were *"550 at Mukti who met twice a day to pray for revival."*

The Holy Spirit was about to move with extraordinary power among that group of once-neglected and helpless widows. A date that is remembered by Christians in India is June 29, 1905, a day of awe. God opened the heavens and came down. It started out slowly and then built to a loud cadence, the sound of large groups of women travailing in the Lord. Weeping and groaning, the women confessed their sins and prayed for on empowerment of God. The next day, Ramabai was preaching from John 8, when suddenly with the sound of a loud rushing wind the Holy Spirit fell upon them. David Smithers writes:

> *"All the women and girls began to weep and confess their sins. Many were stricken down under conviction of sin while out attending to their daily studies and household duties. Lessons were suspended and the women gave themselves to continual prayer. During these days of heart-searching repentance, many girls had visions of the 'body of sin' within themselves. They testified that the Holy Spirit came into them with a holy burning, which they called a baptism of fire that was almost unbearable."*

Of this revival, one reporter stated:

> *"The girls in India so wonderfully wrought upon and baptized with the Holy Spirit… were under a pungent conviction of their need. Great light was given them. When delivered they jumped up and down for joy for hours without fatigue. They cried out with the burning that came into and upon them, while the fire of God burned the members of the body of sin, pride, anger, love of the world, selfishness,*

uncleanness, etc. They neither ate nor slept until the victory was won. Then the joy was so great that for two or three days after receiving the baptism of the Holy Spirit they did not care for food."

After spending some time at Mukti observing the revival, G.H. Lang wrote:

"Little girls were lost for hours in the transport of loving Jesus and praising Him. Young Christians were counting it a rare privilege to spend many successive hours in intercessory prayer for strangers never seen or known... In one meeting we were seventeen hours together; the following day more than fifteen hours passed before the meeting broke up with great joy."

In the biography of Pandita Ramabai, Dr. Nicol MacNicol wrote, *"Those who seemed to have such emotional blessings at the time of the revival were still living steadfast, godly lives twenty years later."*

A well-known minister once told E.M Bounds:

"I have seen God's hand stretched out to heal among the heathen in as mighty wonder-

working power as in apostolic times. I was preaching to two thousand starving orphan girls at Kedgaum, India, at Ramabai's Mukti Mission. A swarm of serpents, as venomous and deadly as the reptile that smote Paul, suddenly raided the walled grounds. They were 'sent of Satan,' said Ramabai, and several of her most beautiful and faithful Christian girls were smitten by them. Two of them were bitten twice. I saw four of the very flower of her flock in convulsions at once, unconscious and apparently in the agonies of death. Ramabai believed the Bible with an implicit and obedient faith. There were three of us missionaries there. She said, 'We will do just what the Bible says. I want you to minister for their healing according to James 5:14-18.' She led the way into the dormitory where her girls were lying in spasms and we laid our hands upon their heads and prayed and anointed them with oil in the name of the Lord. Each of them were healed as soon as they were anointed and they all sat up and sang with their faces shining. That miracle and marvel among the heathen mightily confirmed the word of the

Lord and was a profound and overpowering proclamation of God."

Letters and diaries of the women are filled with the testimonies of the Holy Ghost fire that fell upon them, a fire that was almost unbearable as it purged out of them all that was not of Him. God took a woman with an all embracing heart; a woman called the "mother of modern India"; a woman given the honorific title of "Pandita," mistress of wisdom; a woman who, even though she had all the worldly acclaim, knew she lacked this one thing; a woman who in later years prayed, not for the conversion of Hindus but for the conversion of Indian Christians— and armed her with a vision that set her to praying like never before; that the power of God would change the course of a nation and a people. It worked, and He did!

"People must not only hear about the Kingdom of God, but most see it in actual operation, on a small scale perhaps and in imperfect form, but a real demonstration nevertheless."

— PANDITA RAMABAI

Ramabai died on April 5, 1922, at the age of sixty-four.

Vishal Mangalwadi, an international renowned scholar and author comments:

"There are good reasons to nominate Mrs. Indira Gandhi as the Indian Woman of the 20th Century. However, had she been born a century earlier, she would have been married off to a Hindu Brahmin as an illiterate girl before she was 12 years old. And had she refused to be burnt alive on her husbands' funeral pyre, she would have to spend her widowhood in seclusion as an inauspicious woman. The woman who began reforming India's attitude towards women was Pandita Ramabai... a builder of modern India. Pandita Ramabai is the Indian woman of the Millennium."

"If My people who are called by My name will humble themselves, and pray and seek My face, and turn from their wicked ways, then I will

hear from heaven, and will forgive their sin and heal their land."

(2 CHRONICLES 7:14)

CHAPTER FOUR

MARIA WOODWORTH-ETTER

"If Jesus had preached the same message that ministers preach today, He would never have been crucified."

— LEONARD RAVENHILL

"We cannot rely on ourselves, for we have learned by bitter experience the folly of self-confidence. We are compelled to look to the Lord alone. Blessed is the wind that drives the ship into the harbor. Blessed is the distress that forces us to rest in our God."

— CHARLES H. SPURGEON

"Begin to rejoice in the Lord, and your bones will flourish like an herb, and your cheeks will glow with the bloom of health and freshness. Worry, fear, distrust, care—all are poisonous!

Joy is balm and healing, and if you will but rejoice, God will give power."

— A. B. SIMPSON

"How sweet the name of Jesus sounds, in a believer's ear! It soothes his sorrows, heals his wounds, and drives away his fear."

— JOHN NEWTON

"Father, I just want to be where you are,
my life is filled with everything but you.
Lord, I really want to see Your Glory.
Let the fire of heaven fall on me.
Can you feel my passion, can you see my hunger,
Do you know how I long for you,
No walls between us,
Take away this darkness,
Come break this heart of stone;
Hear my cry… Open up the sky!"

— LINDELL COOLEY

Roberts Liardon, in his book *God's Generals*, writes this about Maria (pronounced *Ma-ri-ah*, not *Ma-ree-ah*) Woodworth-Etter:

> *"There hasn't been a greater demonstrator of God's Spirit since the book of Acts in Pentecostal history than Maria Woodworth-Etter. She was an incredible woman of vision and spiritual strength who stood in the face of fierce opposition, lifted her tiny hand, and allowed the Holy Spirit to spread His fire. Sister Etter lived in the realm of the spirit as a powerful vessel of God's divine leading and His supernatural manifestations."*

It was October 1857, and the "Third Great Awakening" was sweeping though America. The country was, once again, being touched by the Spirit of God. Churches everywhere were being shaken by a revival of prayer never before seen in Church history. 10,000 people in New York City alone gathered together daily, even left work, to pray. The same thing was taking place all over the country, in small towns as well as great cities. The "Awakening" was even spreading into Canada where groups of 5,000 or more were attending camp meetings daily in Ontario and Quebec. That is what was happening in the Kingdom of God, but in the world it was a different story. A national financial crisis was occurring, with bank failures, railroads going into bankruptcy, and financial chaos arising everywhere. Civil War was just over the horizon, and America tottered on the brink of disaster.

In a small church in New Lisbon, Ohio, a young thirteen-year-old girl was so taken aback by what was being preached that everything in her was shaking. At the call for repentance she rushed to the altar and gave her life to God, being "Born Again." The preacher who led her to the Lord prayed that her life "might be a shining light." God answered that prayer in abundance. That young girl would become a powerful voice in the Pentecostal movement. She would become the legendary evangelist who worked many "signs and wonders," Maria Woodworth-Etter.

Maria would always remember the voice of God she heard deep in her spirit that day:

> *"I heard the voice of Jesus calling me to go out in the highways and hedges and gather in the lost sheep."*

One fact kept her from fulfilling that calling: In the mid1800s there was no room for women preachers. At that time in Church history, women, for the most part, were not allowed in the pulpit. So even though God said to go, she stayed in her role, not wanting to be frowned upon or ostracized by the church leadership.

She settled into what she thought was a normal Christian lifestyle of marriage and having children. In 1863, Philo Horace Woodworth was discharged from the Union Army with a head wound. Living in the same town, Maria and Philo soon met, courted, and married. The marriage would produce six children, of which Maria poured her love into, only to watch as five would die from a terrible disease. Still that voice deep inside was calling her to the ministry. Her excuse this time was the necessities of marriage and a grieving husband who never would get over the death of the children. She became frustrated with her role as a wife and mother because she could not answer the call to preach. Another drawback she was facing was that her husband had no desire for ministry.

Through it all she never lost her desire for a sincere walk with God. She would fight to find time to read and study the Word of God. It was at this time she had a vision that changed her life. Angels came into her room and:

> *"They took her to the West, over prairies, lakes, forests, and rivers where she saw a long, wide field of waving golden grain. As the view unfolded she began to preach and saw the grains begin to fall like sheaves. Then Jesus told her that, 'just as the grain fell, so people would fall' as she preached."*

The vision was so real that immediately she cast out the fear of man and answered the call of God upon her life. She would preach no matter what the fathers of the church would say. She asked God to anoint her with great power and she then dedicated her life to Him.

The presence of the Lord was with Maria from the first. Her first preaching engagement was to a small group of people, mostly relatives, gathered in a meeting room. Maria began preaching and immediately the crowd began to be consumed by the Holy Spirit, many weeping and falling to the floor. Some got up and ran out the door in tears, unable to stand in the glorified presence of God.

It wasn't long before churches from all over began asking her to come and revive their congregations. She traveled out West and held nine revivals, amazingly with no ministerial training at all. Over a short time she preached 200 sermons and started two churches with memberships of over 100 people each. God had called her years before, but now He was redeeming the time, and in one town the entire population cried and repented before the Lord. Believe it or not, that town's name was "Devils Den" and Maria brought the greatest manifestation of the presence of God the town had ever witnessed.

Her ministry was not just words of human wisdom but was in the demonstration of the Spirit and of power (1 Corinthians 2:4). And it is there that she suffered fierce persecution. You see, the Church throughout history has always been quick to judge something it did not understand, mostly because it has lost so much of the power the first Church lived and walked in. The manifestations that today's Church ridicules were common occurrences to first century Christians. Many talk against signs and wonders because it eases their conscience and allows them the safety of leading a less then holy life (Leviticus 11:44, 45; 1Peter 1:16). Many Christians walk far beneath the calling they have from Jesus (Mark 16: 17-18). Many are hiding behind the conscience-soothing "doctrine" of Dispensationalism, the belief that the gifts and signs from God ended with the Apostles, that God was more faithful with one generation than He was with another. That is not Scriptural. The Bible says, *"Jesus Christ is the same yesterday, today and forever" (Hebrews 13:8).* He and His promises never change. Everything He speaks in His Word is for today's Christians as well as yesterday's, *"For the gifts and the calling of God are irrevocable" (Romans 11:29).* Scripture also tells us how Paul and the Apostles passed the power of the Holy Spirit, including the signs and wonders, to other believers and gentiles (Acts 10:44-47; 19:1-6). These believers then passed the same Gifts of the Spirit to others from generation to generation (for more documentation of this, read early Christian historian Eucebius's account of the power within the Church). Through the centuries men began to place more trust in their own righteousness and more faith in their own selves, the created instead of He who was the Creator, and lost the anointing that is so needed in today's society (Romans 1:25).

Maria opened the door and pioneered the way for the Pentecostal manifestations that are so prominent in that movement today. She preached in meetings sponsored by Methodists, United Brethren, Churches of God, Presbyterian, and others. In all those meetings she stressed the baptism in the "Holy Ghost." During an 1883 meeting in Fairview, Ohio, Maria wrote that as the people confessed sin and prayed for a baptism of the Holy Ghost and fire:

> *"Fifteen came to the altar screaming for mercy. Men and women fell and lay like dead. I had never seen anything like this. I felt it was the work of God, but did not know how to explain it, or what to say."*

While Maria was lost for an explanation, the Bible explains it best (Matthew 28:4; John 18:6; Rev 1:17).

During that service those who were laying on the floor for some time, slain in the Spirit, would then arise with praises to the Lord God Almighty on their tongues, and the ministers and elders all wept and praised God for His presence and power. Not only would people drop over "as if dead," but they would also stagger about as if they had too much to drink

(Acts 2:15). Word spread, and at one meeting fifteen doctors came to investigate and expose this phenomenon of "His Pentecost Power." The leader of the group was a world-class leader in his field. Maria wrote of that meeting:

> *"He did not want to admit the power was of God. He would have been glad if they could prove it was something else. He came to investigate... to his surprise he found his son at the altar and wanted his father to pray for him. He could not pray. God showed him what he was and what he was doing. He began to pray for himself. While praying he fell [in the Spirit] and saw the horrors of hell. He was falling in... God saved him. He went on to work to win souls for Christ."*

Another man, full of a religious spirit, witnessed the meeting and made some joking remark concerning the display of power. Filled with religious pride, he boldly headed toward the platform to investigate and expose this nonsense. Before he reached the front, he was *"struck to the floor by the power of God"* and laid there for over two hours. When he came back to his senses, he was born again with his life forever changed. He later was quoted as saying:

> *"He regretted having spent sixty years lost in religion, never knowing the real Jesus Christ personally."*

Liardon writes:

> *"Still newspapers and unbelieving ministers warned others to stay away from the meetings. They said they 'would make a person insane.' Nevertheless, thousands were saved, many being 'struck down, laying as dead men' even on their way home. It is said many fell under the power in their homes, miles away from the meetings."*

Maria believed in worshipping God totally, like King David did, with all that is within us, including dancing, shouting, and singing because He deserved nothing less. If one can go and act "the fool" at a sporting event, he can worship his God with the same passion.

Wherever she preached, people from all walks of life were saved. Entire towns changed personality.

After one of her meetings in 1885, the police had never seen such a change in their city. They actually had nothing to do. The manifestations of the Holy Ghost that followed her ministry were always followed by hundreds coming to Christ. She allowed the Holy Spirit complete freedom in her meetings, refusing to let the spirit of control take over by limiting the time of worship or the time of the service. Sometimes a meeting was all worship, sometimes all prayer, and she fought the desire to preach, not because it was wrong but because the Spirit was moving then among the people. Time would come to preach and there were meetings of just preaching. In every meeting signs and wonders in the form of manifestations of the Spirit were prevalent. Maria looked at these as:

"Nothing new; they were just something the Church had lost."

Once in a meeting a crowd rushed the platform to seek God, Maria raised her hand, wanting to pray, and:

"They went down [fell] by the mighty wind of the power of God... hundreds of sinners received the gift of eternal life."

Twenty-five thousand people crowded into one meeting place. A reporter wrote:

> *"Vehicles of all sorts began pouring into the city at an early hour—nothing short of a circus or a political rally ever before brought in so large a crowd."*

Before Maria finished preaching, the power of God fell on the large gathering and took control of about five hundred as they fell to the ground. When they came to, all, in unison, glorified God and gave their lives to Jesus.

Another move of God through the ministry of Maria was the healing of the sick. She studied His divine will in healing and together working hand-in-hand with the *"Lord that heals you" (Exodus 15:26)*, thousands were won to Christ as a result of seeing others healed. Another "healing" evangelist at that time, John Alexander Dowie, was quite annoyed at her ministry encroaching on his territory and began to publicly blast and defame her, calling all she did as a "great delusion." Maria never said a harsh word against him or his ministry, telling those concerned that she *"would leave him in the hands of God and that I would go right on with the Master… and that I would be living when he was dead."* Soon Dowie's ministry fell in disgrace and Maria outlived him by seventeen years.

The enemy tried to do all he could to put an end to Maria's ministry. Failing in his attempt to eliminate her from the inside by using the self-righteous and religious people in the Church, he changed tactics and decided to use his own people. During a Crusade in Oakland, California, ruffians, hoodlums, and gang members started harassing her meetings by shouting obscene language and throwing explosives among the people. Miraculously, no one was ever injured. She received death threats constantly and newspapers slandered her relentlessly. The Oakland Police Department deputized "bouncers" to protect the services, but in most cases they were as bad in character as those who were causing the disturbances. Maria never wavered but kept on preaching:

> *"I have been in great dangers; many times not knowing when I would be shot down, either in the pulpit, or going to and from meetings… But I said I would never run, nor compromise. The Lord would always put His mighty power on me, so that He took all fear away, and made me*

like a giant... If in any way they had tried to shoot, or kill me, He would have struck them dead, and I sometimes told them so."

Those who came to investigate, condemn, or harass her seemed most at risk of "falling out" or being "slain in the Spirit." One man came to a meeting intent on disrupting it. He got within ten feet of the platform and let out a stream of vulgarity and cursing. Then suddenly his voice just faded away as a *"strange power seemed to grip his vocal chords."* Two newspaper reporters who were there to write about the meeting asked the disturbed man why his voice died away, and the man, still shaking from the experience, said, *"Go up there yourself and find out and feel that power."* One night three well-respected, dignified ministers walked into a meeting intent on getting to the bottom of these "heresies" that were befalling the people. They were going to *"set matters right."* The room was so full there wasn't a seat in the house. Being well-known in the area, three platform preachers gave up their seats behind Maria. The stuffy ministers reluctantly took the seats. Maria started the service and the power of God fell upon the place. Suddenly one of the ministers fell off his chair into the sawdust on the floor and lay motionless. The other two tried to ignore what had happened when a second minister fell in the "Spirit" and landed beside the other on the floor. Soon the third fell off the platform and all three were like "dead men" as they were laid out under the power of God for over three hours. Then finally one by one they got up and walked in a daze toward the exit.

At the peak of her ministry news of the unfaithfulness of her husband became known. Unwillingness to quit his infidelity and change his ways forced Maria to get a divorce in January 1891. Less than a year later, he remarried and began to publicly slander Maria's character. Within a few weeks he was dead of Typhoid Fever. Ten years later she met a godly man, Samuel Etter, and they were married. Samuel became a vital part of the ministry and together they preached and labored for the Lord until he died twelve years later. Maria referred to him as her *"gift from God"*:

> *"He stood bravely with me in the hottest battle, and since the day we were married had never shrank. He will defend the Word and all the gifts, and operations of the Holy Ghost, but does not want any fanaticism, or foolishness. It*

makes no difference what I call on him to do. He will pray, and preach, and sing, and is very good around the altar. The Lord knew what I needed, and it was all brought about by the Lord, through His love and care for me and the work."

It is amazing that throughout her ministry the critics were many. But when you follow their trails you see where God silenced them all.

As the turn of the century passed, her fame for miraculous healing and revival services grew. It wasn't rare for some people to carry their sick over two thousand miles to a healing meeting. Doctors became a common sight at her meetings and many of the healings were documented and attested to by these notable physicians. The *Topeka Capitol* newspaper had this headline from a 1915 meeting in Topeka, Kansas: *"Boy Cured by Miracle,"* referring to a 10-year-old boy Louis Romer. He was suffering with what was known as St. Vitus' dance (chorea). Louis said he shook so badly he couldn't feed himself, and his toes bent under his feet, preventing him from wearing shoes. When in his 90s and living in Lowell, Oregon, he remembered that summer night long ago:

"Sister Etter laid her hands on my head, and I felt a cooling of my nerves as a tingling warmth went through my body. Then before my eyes my hands and feet straightened. I felt so good I just cried and cried and cried. The terrible shaking stopped immediately and in all these years has never come back. All this happened in less time than it takes for me to tell it."

The first thing Louis and his mother did was to go out and buy him his first pair of shoes.

Documented cases by doctors included invalids walking from their sick beds, the deaf hearing, the blind seeing, arthritis healing instantly, tumors being destroyed, and the disease of dropsy being eliminated, all in the name of Jesus. Maria was emphatic about not taking any credit for what she did not do; it was the Hand of God.

One man had three broken ribs from a fall and could hardly stand because of the pain. Maria laid her hands on him and offered the prayer of faith. As she touched him he flinched, then he began pounding on his healed rib cage shouting that the pain was gone. Another man had a hopeless case of tuberculosis and was also plagued with an open sore that left a deep hole in his body. The power of God fell on him through the laying on of hands, and he jumped off his cot and ran up and down the aisle in front of the crowd. A man was cured of cancer on his face and neck. It disappeared in front of everyone. He then jumped up on the altar and preached to the people. Three women were cured from being deaf and dumb. One of the ladies remembers:

> *"When Sister Etter put her finger in my mouth at the root of my tongue and then in my ears, commanding in the name of Jesus that a 'deaf and dumb' spirit come out, God instantly opened my ears and gave me my voice!"*

F.F. Bosworth, the great healing evangelist and pastor, wrote about visiting one of Maria's healing services:

> *"Night after night, as soon as the invitation was given, all the available space around the fifty-foot altar would be filled with so many suffering with diseases and afflictions and others seeking salvation and the baptism in the Holy Ghost, that it was difficult to get in and out among the seekers."*

The healing of a young boy with a tumor the size of a fist is still talked about in West Indianapolis. The boy's mother helped him up on the platform and Maria said, *"We will just cut it out with the Sword of the Spirit."* With that, Maria took her Bible and "whacked" the boy on the neck and he was healed instantly. That boy grew up to become a well know evangelist by the name of Roscoe Russell.

By 1912, Maria was fully part of the new Pentecostal Movement, saying that:

> *"It was the greatest thing to happen to the Church since the Day of Pentecost."*

After forty-five years of ministry and thousands and thousands of healings, Maria decided to build a church next door to her home in Indianapolis, Indiana. The church would seat 500 and she called it "The Tabernacle." For the last six years of her life she would minister there. The church still remains today and is affiliated with the Assemblies of God under the name Lakeview Temple.

Marie repeatedly said during her ministry that she would *"sooner wear out for Jesus than rust out."* She was faithful to that saying by preaching and healing up to her last days. In 1924, at the age of eighty, Maria Woodworth-Etter fell into a deep sleep and went to be with her Lord.

There is a quote from Maria in an Illinois newspaper dated 1885 that maybe will free many from the deception that keeps them from walking in the fullness of the Spirit:

> *"The power which was given to the apostles in their day had never been taken from the Church. The trouble was, the churches had sunk to the level of the world and were without the unlimited faith that will heal the sick and make the lame to walk. I pray for the return of the old days and more faith in Christ among the people.*

> *"If I do not do the works of My Father, do not believe Me. But if I do, though you do not believe Me, believe the works, that you may know and believe that the Father is in Me, and I in Him."*

(JOHN 10:37-38)

CHAPTER FIVE

AMY CARMICHAEL

"We must be global Christians with a global vision because our God is a global God."

— JOHN STOTT

"I have but one candle of life to burn, and I would rather burn it out in a land filled with darkness than in a land flooded with light."

— JOHN KEITH FALCONER

"We shall have all eternity in which to celebrate our victories, but we have only one swift hour before the sunset in which to win them."

— ROBERT MOFFATT

"The Spirit of Christ is the spirit of missions. The nearer we get to Him, the more intensely missionary we become."

— HENRY MARTYN

In God's kingdom some are called to be apostles, some prophets, some evangelists, and some pastors and teachers. (Ephesians 4:12) Out of these offices, some are called, by God, to have great healing ministries, some to be great worship leaders, some to be leaders of large churches, some to bring revival to nations, others to local congregations. Some are called to stand strong and be a hedge between the prince of this world, the devil, and those who are needy, innocent, and hurting. This was the call on Amy Wilson Carmichael.

Amy Carmichael was born December 16, 1867 and died January 18, 1951 at the age of 83. In between she led a long and fruitful life of service to the Lord. Amy was a protestant Christian missionary in India, Japan and China. She opened an orphanage and founded a mission in Dohnavur, India and saved thousands of pre-teen girls from a life of religious prostitution. She served in India for 56 years without one day of vacation and also authored many books about her missionary works. Amy's parents, David and Catherine Carmichael, were devout Presbyterians and lived in the small village of Millisle, Northern Ireland.

Amy was the oldest of seven children. The family owned flour mills and were very wealthy. Her early years were quite comfortable lacking nothing. Even from her early years, Christian principles were instilled in Amy and as early as she could remember, she always had a trust in God. One of the first recorded incidents that occurred when she was a child is amusing. Her mother had said that whatever Amy prayed for God would answer. Amy had brown eyes, she then prayed for blue. The next morning she jumped out of bed and ran to the mirror, then cried out in disappointment. After a while her mother finally convinced Amy that "no" also was an answer from God. Her mother explained that God meant for Amy to have brown eyes for a reason (as we will find out later in this story). Just what that reason was, her mother continued, she might never know. Until then, her mother stated, remember, brown eyes were perfectly lovely. Amy remembers thinking that she wasn't so sure. Smiling, Amy thought, royal blue would always be her favorite color, even if God did say "no."

On another occasion, Amy was outside on a bitter cold day and found a frozen mouse. She couldn't help but feel compassion for the stiff little creature, but it was time for family devotion, so she rushed inside so she would not be late. After a short while small squeaks began to interrupt the family prayers. As questions arose, as to what and where was that sound, Amy looked around innocently not letting on that the frozen mouse in her pocket had revived. Amy was quite precocious and one time led her brothers and sisters in a challenge to see how many poisonous laburnum pods they could eat before they died. Fortunately, all they got were severe upset stomachs.

Amy was eighteen years old when her father died. His death resulted in financial trouble for the family. At that time they were forced to move to Belfast. It was here that God touched Amy while she was working for city missions. All through her youth, Amy thought she was a "real Christian," but an evangelist showed her that she needed a personal commitment to Jesus. She then, without hesitation, gave her heart fully to Christ. Service to Him became the center and passion of her life. One day Amy, and her mother, went to buy a dress. Amy found a beautiful one—royal blue—but turned away from it. This surprised her mother, but Amy explained that clothes were no longer important to her, as they once were, now that Jesus had given her a new purpose in life.

Amy, the future missionary, got her first taste for that life on the streets of Belfast. She started Bible classes and prayer groups for the poor and destitute of the city. She also began a Sunday club consisting of classes for a group of ladies called "Shawlies." These were factory girls that were so poor they could not afford hats to wear to church so they wore shawls instead. (Editor's note: In those days' women always wore a head covering when they entered a church sanctuary. [1 Corinthians 11:2-16] This practice still continues with many groups but mostly fell out of favor in the 1960s.) The "well to do" and the "respectable" ladies usually wanted nothing to do with the "shawlies." Amy knew that they needed Christ just the same as their supposed "betters" so she started the classes. At first, only a half dozen attended, but before long Amy had to find a place large enough to hold three hundred or more. However, during this time the financial pressure increased on her family. Mrs. Carmichael was forced to move the family to England and begin working for her late husband's brother. Amy was put to work immediately, when Uncle Jacob asked her to teach his mill workers about Christ. Amy did not hesitate; she moved into a cockroach and bed bug-infested apartment near the mill and set up classes. It wasn't long before she was breathing new life into those workers, both men and women. It was during this time that a desire began burning in her heart to enter the mission field. Amy later attended a convention in 1883 where she heard Hudson Taylor speak about the missionary life. It was then that she was convinced that her calling was to the same labor. Amy told some friends that the desire to become a missionary was so strong, in her, that it hurt. She prayed constantly about it and wrote down the reasons she thought it couldn't possibly be God's intention for her.

One of the first things on her list was her "sickness." Amy suffered from neuralgia, a disease of the nerves that made her whole body weak and achy and often put her in bed for weeks on end. When she was at prayer about it, she heard the Lord say *"GO"* so she replied *"surely, Lord, you do not mean it."* Again, the voice said, *"GO"* and from that time on, for her, there was no turning back.

Her unwavering determination to put God before everything else soon began to mark her ministry. On March 3, 1893, she set sail for Japan with three other women missionaries. Amy had a constant passion to witness for Christ and she took advantage of every opportunity no matter where it showed itself. Before the ship she was sailing on made it to port the captain was converted by her love for Jesus. Immediately upon arriving in Japan, even before she learned the language, Amy was out witnessing with an interpreter by the name of Miseki Ian. A writer for the "Christian History Institute" reports:

"Once when Amy was about to visit the Buddhist village of Hirose she felt impressed of the Lord to pray for one soul. A young silk weaver was open to her message and became a Christian. Amy's neuralgia kept her in bed for a month after that. The next time she went out she prayed for two souls. The silk weaver brought two friends, they accepted Jesus. Two weeks later Amy felt impressed to ask for four souls. That was more souls than any of the missionaries saw won to Christ in a year. The meeting started badly. Not many came to the service and those few that did seemed distracted. Suddenly the spirit in the room changed and a

woman spoke up and asked the way to Christ,
then her son and later two other women."

Amy was sick again for a month and a half. During that time the Lord said she should pray for eight souls. When she shared her goal with the other missionaries, they chided her. *"It is not faith,"* they said, *"but presumption."* With astonishment Amy heard them advise her just to pray for a blessing, *"'then you will not be disappointed.' Amy told them that this was from the Lord because she could never accomplish this in her own strength. An older missionary agreed with her and they both prayed together. And then, to the shock of all, eight souls gave their all to Christ."*

Amy had her eyes opened wide in regard to those called to missions. She expected everyone's heart to be totally sold out to Christ; her introduction to missionary life was a disappointment. The main problem, as she saw it, was that the missionaries were no different than the men and women they were sent to convert. She wrote:

"...We are here just what we are at home—not one bit better—and the devil is awfully busy...

there are many missionary shipwrecks of once fair vessels."

Her desire to live a pure life before God and to bring that light to the world pushed her away from her fellow missionaries in Japan. Frustrated, she came back home to take care of a sick friend. The call of missions was so strong that in less than a year, Amy was back in the mission field. This time she chose India.

Amy once said, *"You can give without loving. But you cannot love without giving."* She lived it, especially when it came to children. Her main accomplishment on the mission field in India was saving the "temple children." This was one of the "secret sins" of Hinduism, and it was Amy who saved those children from becoming temple prostitutes. These temple children were young girls dedicated to the gods and forced into prostitution to earn money for the priests. Amy uncovered this abomination through the help of converted Indian women. She founded an organization known as the Dohnavur fellowship. This group soon became the sanctuary for more than one thousand children who would have, otherwise, faced a dark future. Amy put her whole heart into the struggle to end this wicked practice. To "kidnap" these girls, Amy would pretend to be an Indian and visit the temple. She would stain her skin with coffee and wear Indian clothing to pass as a Hindu. Now she finally understood why God had given her brown eyes. Those blue eyes she prayed for long ago would have been a dead giveaway. One of the characteristics of the fellowship was everyone wore Indian dress and the children were given Indian names and were all told about their Savior, Jesus Christ. Amy cared for the spiritual and physical needs of these precious girls claiming, *"one saves and then pitchforks souls into heaven... souls are more or less securely fashioned to bodies... and as you cannot get the souls out and deal with them separately, you have to take them both together."*

Nothing could stop her from telling anyone, anywhere about the love of Jesus. Amy often traveled long distances on India's hot and dusty roads to save one child from suffering. One of Amy's rescues was five year old Kahila. This young girl was abused daily and her guardians wanted her back. Amy refused to return the little girl to that certain abuse. Instead she made plans to cause the girl to "disappear" to a safe place. Amy was too well known to do it herself. So she arranged for someone else to do it. The plot was discovered anyway. Charges were brought against Amy for kidnapping. Amy was facing a seven year prison term. But instead, on February 7, 1914, a telegram arrived saying, *"criminal case dismissed."* No explanation was ever forthcoming, but Amy and those who knew her Lord suspected He had a hand in the decision.

In 1931, Amy was badly injured in a fall, which left her bedridden for twenty years until her death in 1951 at the age of 83. She asked that no stone be put over her grave, instead the girls she cared for put a bird bath over it with a single inscription *"Amma,"* which means *mother* in Tamil.

God used Amy's compassion for the needy and hurting in a powerful way.

"But Jesus said, 'Let the little children come to me, and do not forbid them; for such is the kingdom of Heaven.'"

(MATTHEW 19:14)

Chapter Six

Kathryn Kuhlman

"…The atonement of Christ lays the foundation equally for deliverance from sin and… from disease… Complete provision has been made for both… in the exercise of faith… We have the same reason to believe that the body may be delivered from sickness that we have that the soul may be delivered from sin."

— DR. R. E. STANTON

"I am the Lord who heals you."

— YAHWEH RAPHA (EXODUS 23:24)

"He who waives away the healing power of Christ as belonging only to the New Testament times is not preaching the whole gospel. God was and is the Saviour of the body as well as the soul."

— BISHOP CHARLES H. BRENT

"God wants to take natural people and work supernaturally through them to bring about a mighty surge of His power…"

— LESTER SUMRALL

"Time… is slipping by, and your opportunity will soon be gone. Look at that poor wretch groveling in the mire of sin: he needs to be told of the power of God to save. Look at that dear saint agonizing in the languishing bed of sickness; she needs to hear of the power of God to heal."

— GEORGE JEFFREYS

"Who forgives all your iniquities, Who heals all your diseases."

— KING DAVID (PSALM 103:3)

It was 1976, and Oral Roberts was at the Forest Lawn Memorial Park presiding over the funeral of this special woman of God. While he was speaking he had a vision that God would raise up and spread similar ministries throughout the world, making the magnitude of God's power greater than He did through this woman's life. But Kathryn Kuhlman had a special calling. She showed an entire generation how to love and have fellowship with the Holy Spirit. She revealed the Holy Spirit as a friend and His purpose was to point us to Jesus. She dedicated her entire life to "one whom I've never seen." Over the years her ministry would shift the focus of the Church from the outward show of supernatural gifts of the Holy Spirit back to the Giver of the gifts. Kathryn walked in the authority of what the Church will be like in times to come, a forerunner of the true "Bride of Christ."

Roberts Liardon, in his book *Kathryn Kuhlman: A Spiritual Biography of God's Miracle Working Power,* writes about a Kuhlman meeting:

> *"Hundreds have been healed just sitting quietly in the audience without any demonstration whatsoever. None. Very often not even a sermon is preached. There have been times when not even a song has been sung. No loud demonstration, no loud calling on God as though He were deaf. No screaming, no shouting, within the very quietness of His presence. There were hundreds of times when*

the presence of the Holy Spirit was so real that one could almost hear the rhythm as thousands of hearts beat as one."

Kathryn manifested the power of the Holy Spirit wherever she went. No matter how large or tall a building was, sinner or saint always knew when Kathryn entered the building, because the whole atmosphere seemed to change. Her life was a commitment to prayer. Traveling constantly, she prayed continuously. Before her meetings, her staff relates that Kathryn could be seen *"pacing back and forth, head up, head down, arms flung into the air, hands clasped behind her back with her face covered in tears."* Oral Roberts tells us of the intensity of her prayers, *"It was like they were talking back and forth to each other, and you couldn't tell where Kathryn started and the Holy Spirit left off. It was a oneness."*

Kathryn was born May 9, 1907. Her parents, Joseph Adolph and Emma Walkenhorst Kuhlman, were German immigrants and living on a farm outside of Concordia, Missouri. Her mother was Methodist and her father was Baptist. Her mother was a church member but her father had a strong aversion to preachers, saying that they *"were in it for the money,"* and refused to even walk on the same side of the street as they did. As far as Kathryn knew, he never prayed or read the Bible. A childhood friend describes Kathryn as having:

> "Large features, red hair, and freckles. It could not be said of Kathryn that she was pretty. She was not dainty or appealing feminine in any sense of the word. She was taller than the rest of 'our gang' [five foot eight], gangly and boyish in build, and her long strides kept the rest of us puffing to keep up with her."

From early in her life Kathryn felt the urgings of the Spirit. She believed that church attendance was just as important as going to work, and at the age of 14 in her mother's Methodist church she gave her life to God:

> "I was standing beside Mama… I can't remember the minister's name or even one word of his sermon, but something happened to me… As I stood there, I began shaking to the extent that I could no longer hold the hymnal, so I laid it on the pew… and sobbed. I was feeling the weight of (conviction) and I realized that I was

a sinner. I felt like the meanest, lowest person in the whole world... I did the only thing I knew to do: I slipped out from where I was standing and walked to the front pew and sat down in the corner... and wept. Oh, how I wept! I had become the happiest person in the whole world. The heavy weight had been lifted. I experienced something that has never left me. I had been born again, and the Holy Spirit had done the very thing that Jesus said He would do. (John 16:8)"

In 1922, the Kuhlman family was registered as members of the local Baptist church. In her early years Kathryn went to a Baptist seminary and was ordained as a Baptist preacher. In her later years Kathryn refused to be part of any denomination and gave no organization any credit for her ministry, only God.

Later, Myrtle and Everett Parrott, her sister and brother-in-law, invited her to travel with them and preach at their tent revivals. She stayed with them from the age of sixteen until she was twenty-one. During the time she spent with the Parrotts, they were influenced by Dr. Charles S. Price, a Canadian evangelist, who instructed Parrott on the baptism in the Holy Spirit. This was when the healing ministry was introduced into their revivals. While with the Parrotts, Kathryn also attended the Simpson Bible School in Seattle for two years.

When Kathryn was twenty-one, she started her own ministry. Her first mission was a small dirty pool hall in Boise, Idaho. From the pool hall she went to an old filthy opera house that she had to clean and make ready for her evangelistic meetings. Nothing deterred her as she became well-known, traveling and preaching in tents and barns in Idaho, Utah, and Colorado. Many times she did not know where she would spend the night. On one occasion, the family with whom she was scheduled to stay only had a turkey house that they scrubbed clean for her. In those days guest rooms rarely had heat and Kathryn remembers snuggling under great piles of covers until she got the spot warm where she lay. Then she would turn over on her stomach and study the Word of God for hours at a time.

> *"...My heart is fixed. I'll be loyal to Him at any cost, at any price. Loyalty is much more than a casual interest in someone or something. It's a personal commitment. In the final analysis, it*

means, 'Here I am. You can count on me. I won't fail you.'"

After a six-month revival in Pueblo, Colorado, Kathryn moved to Denver and opened her own church in an old Montgomery Ward warehouse, calling it the Denver Revival Tabernacle. The first night, 125 people were present; the second night, over 400; and from then on the warehouse was filled to capacity every night. A larger meeting place was found that held over 2,000 people, and over the years the building was consistently filled. Services were held every night except Monday.

During this time, a traveling evangelist, Burroughs A. Waltrip from Austin, Texas, was invited to speak at the church. He was married but told everyone that his wife had left him and, through no fault of his own, asked for a divorce. The truth was the opposite; he had left her and it would be awhile before that would come to light. In the meantime Waltrip and Kathryn found themselves attracted to each other and soon married. It wasn't long after that the truth came out and Kathryn left him, but it cost her "the ministry" she had so devoutly built. She never again saw Waltrip and soon left for Franklin,

Pennsylvania, to start her life again preaching the Word of her Lord.

In Franklin she found people hungry for the gospel. She preached in the 1,500-seat Gospel Tabernacle, made famous since Billy Sunday preached there. Kathryn's ministry there was followed by *"miracles, signs, and wonders."* She would write about those meetings:

> *"Hundreds have been healed just sitting quietly in the audience, without any demonstration whatsoever, and even without admonition... because by His Presence alone, sick bodies are healed."*

Word soon spread throughout the country and "healing meetings" were held wherever she went.

Critics are want to claim that Kathryn's ministry then took a wrong turn, saying it no longer had the saving of souls as its primary focus. This is far from the truth, as we see from Kathryn's own words:

> *"Healing is marvelous, but the greatest miracle is the transformation of a soul from darkness to light. I do not care if I never see another body healed, as long as I know that there are souls*

*being saved. Healing of the body is nothing
compared to the healing of the soul."*

Kathryn believed that healing was provided for the
believer at the same time as salvation. As she was
teaching one night on the Holy Spirit, healings began
in the congregation without her even knowing it until
the next night. It happened by the power of the Holy
Spirit. The next night a woman stood and gave a
testimony about the preceding meeting the night
before. Without anyone laying hands on her and
without Kathryn even being aware of what was
happening, the woman was healed of a cancerous
tumor. The woman had gone to her doctor to confirm
her healing before the evening service. A World War I
veteran, who was blind from the War, received his
sight.

Once the healings and miracles began to take
place, the crowds became even larger. Kathryn would
not take credit for any of them; she would give God
all the glory for the results. A former secretary
remembered:

*"Miss Kuhlman was so tender toward God. I
was standing in the Tabernacle after a service*

*and could see into her room. There was Miss
Kuhlman, unaware that anyone could see her,
on her knees praising God for the service."*

She held a meeting in Carnegie Hall in Pittsburgh, a
meeting place that not even the most popular opera
stars could fill to capacity. The first night, because
every seat in the house was filled, chairs had to be
brought in from elsewhere. Healings took place
throughout the auditorium while people sat in their
seats, looking toward Heaven and focusing on Jesus.
After the meeting people urged her to move her
ministry to Pittsburgh permanently. Kathryn was
reluctant and finally decided against the move:

*"No! The roof on Faith Temple literally would
have to cave in before I'd believe God wanted
me to move to Pittsburgh."*

The next week, on Thanksgiving, 1950, the temple
roof fell in under the weight of the biggest snowfall to
hit that area in its history. Kathryn moved to
Pittsburgh. For the next twenty years she would hold
her famous "miracle services" in Carnegie Hall. People
from all over the world would attend the services. She
conducted an average of 125 healing meetings a year.

She would eventually have national and worldwide radio and television programs to reach millions.

Eventually she moved her meetings from Carnegie Hall to the First Presbyterian Church, and for years these services were attended by some of the most elite Bible scholars in Pittsburgh. These meetings also had an impact on many future evangelists:

> "A friend of mine, Jim Poynter, has asked me to go with him on a… trip to Pittsburgh, Pennsylvania. A group was going to a meeting of a healing evangelist, Kathryn Kuhlman. To be honest, I knew very little about her ministry. I'd seen her on television, and she totally turned me off… I wasn't exactly filled with expectation… We arrived at the First Presbyterian Church… at five in the morning, it was still dark and bitter cold… Hundreds of people were already there… the doors wouldn't open for two more hours. When the doors finally opened it was a race for seats… It would be another hour before the service began… almost out of nowhere, Kathryn Kuhlman appeared. In an instant the atmosphere in that building

became charged... I didn't feel anything around me. No voices. No heavenly angels singing. Nothing. All I knew was that for three hours I would be shaking. It was as if I had exploded... tears streamed down my face... talk about ecstasy! It was a feeling of intense glory... Suddenly I felt a breeze. I looked at the windows but they were all closed. The breeze became more like a wave of wind... I actually felt it moving... the waves of that wind continued to wash over me. And then I felt as if someone had wrapped my body in a... blanket... a blanket of warmth. At that moment I felt... peace... which surpasses all understanding."

— BENNY HINN, HEALING EVANGELIST

Thousands upon thousands of healings took place. People would cram the altar; she would extend her hand toward them and they would fall under the "power of the Holy Ghost," slain in the Spirit. Kathryn offered this explanation:

"All I can believe is that our spiritual beings are not wired for God's full power, and when we

*plug in to that power, we just can't survive it.
We are wired for low voltage; God is high
voltage through the Holy Spirit."*

Kathryn wept for joy as she watched the thousands
being healed through the power of God. She never
tried to explain why some received their healing and
some did not. She believed that the responsibility
remained with God. When a reporter asked her once
why some were not healed, she answered:

*"I do not know, but that will be one of the first
questions I will ask God when I get to heaven!"*

Roberts Lairdon tells us:

*"...A five year old boy, crippled from birth,
walked to Kathryn's platform without
assistance. Another, a woman, who had been
crippled and confined to a wheelchair for twelve
years, walked to the platform without the aid of
her husband. A man... who had received a
pacemaker eight months earlier, felt intense
pain in his chest after Kathryn laid hands on
him. Returning home, he found the scar gone
from his chest where the pacemaker had been*

implanted. Later, when the doctor took X-rays, he discovered the pacemaker was gone and the man's heart healed! It was common for tumors to dissolve, cancers fall off, the blind see, and the deaf to hear. Migraine headaches were healed instantly... It would be impossible to list all the miracles that the ministry of Kathryn Kuhlman witnessed! God alone knows."

In 1952, Kathryn went to Akron, Ohio, to preach, and the police were at their wits end. The meeting was scheduled to start at 11:00 A.M. that morning, and by 4:00 A.M. nearly 18,000 people were gathered around the tent. Kathryn's ministry was known worldwide, and she was even having converts in Hollywood. Top screen stars were coming to her meetings. Even comedienne Phyllis Diller recommended one of Kathryn's books to a dying fan.

Around this time Kathryn was diagnosed as having an enlarged heart and a defective mitral valve. It never stopped her because she was more concerned with the healing of the masses than with her own personal health. Her schedule was extremely hectic and many times she was suffering from physical and mental exhaustion. She continued to minister around the world in Israel, Finland, and Sweden. She was asked to appear on many television shows that were popular at that time, including the Johnny Carson show, Mike Douglas, Merv Griffin, and the Dinah Shore Show.

Her last miracle service was in Los Angeles, California, on November 16, 1975. Three weeks later she lay dying in the Hillcrest Medical Center of Tulsa, Oklahoma, after open-heart surgery. Oral and Evelyn Roberts went to her room to pray for her healing. As they walked toward her bed, Oral remembers:

> *"When Kathryn recognized that we were there to pray for her recovery, she put her hands out like a barrier and then pointed toward heaven."*

Evelyn Roberts looked at her husband and said:

> *"She doesn't want our prayers. She wants to go home."*

The Holy Spirit was in the room with Kathryn, and at the time of her last breath it is said by those present that her face began to shine. Jamie Buckingham, in the book *Daughter of Destiny: Kathryn Kuhlman, Her*

Story, takes us inside Kathryn's hospital room at the time of her death:

> *"The nurse in her room noticed a glow that enveloped her bed, creating an indescribable peace."*

On February 20, 1976, at 8:20 P.M., Kathryn Kuhlman at the age of 68 was granted her wish.

On Kathryn's tombstone in Forest Lawn Memorial Park, Glendale, California, these words are written, *"I believe in miracles, because I believe in God."*

> *"Most assuredly, I say to you, he who believes in Me, the works that I do he will do also; and greater works than these will he do, because I go to My Father."*

(JOHN 14:12)

CHAPTER SEVEN

PEGGY & CHRISTINE SMITH

"To be a Christian without prayer is no more possible than to be alive without breathing."

— MARTIN LUTHER KING JR.

"Prayer is as natural an expression of faith as breathing is to life."

— JONATHAN EDWARDS

"If thou shouldst never see my face again, pray for my soul. More things are wrought by prayer than this world dreams of."

— ALFRED LORD TENNYSEN

"The value of consistent prayer is not that He will hear us, but that we will hear Him."

— WILLIAM MCGILL

*"Some have been to the mountain; I have been
to my knees by the side of my bed."*

— ROBERT BRAULT

*"Prayer does not fit us for the greater work;
prayer is the greater work."*

— OSWALD CHAMBERS

When we think of the Hebrides Revival of 1949-1951
and 1957-1958, we can't help but think of the Great
Evangelist Duncan Campbell who allowed the mighty
presence of the Holy Spirit to flow so freely through
him. But of all revivals, we need to look deeper.
Revival isn't something that just happens to drop out
of Heaven. A true revival is always preceded by
intense intercessory prayer, prevailing prayer, for the
hand of God to sweep through darkness and free the
captives who have been under the oppression of the
devil. It is preceded by prayer warriors travailing day
and night as one given to labor pains. You see, revival
is a birthing.

Charles Finney had his two intercessors that
always preceded him into the city where he was going

to preach. The two precious souls would live in low rent apartments, sometimes even small cramped living quarters in the crawl spaces of houses and would cry out to God to anoint the atmosphere of the surrounding community… preparing the way… making the crooked road straight for what was about to fall out of heaven onto the city. The Hebrides Islands also had their two intercessors, Peggy and Christine Smith.

The Hebrides are a small group of islands off the west coast of Scotland. Peggy and Christine lived all their lives in a small town called Barvas, a small village on the island of Lewis and Harris.

Peggy was 84 years old and blind. Christine was 82 years old and was almost bent double with arthritis. They spoke only their native tongue, which was Gaelic. *"God has chosen the weak things of the world to confound the wise." (1 Corinthians 1:27)* And confound them, they did.

Peggy and Christine spent day and night sending powerful prayers up to the throne for a move of the Spirit in their town. The following is how Leonard Ravenhill documented what happened next. Peggy had heard of how Duncan Campbell was so greatly used of the Lord, that she wrote him a letter asking him to come and preach. He quickly answered back, saying he could not come because of his busy schedule. Peggy and her sister, Christine, pleaded with God day and night for the promise he gave in Isaiah 44:3: *"I will pour water upon him that is thirsty and floods upon a dry ground."* Peggy cried out in her spirit. *"I will not let you go until you bless Barvas!!!"* She sent another letter to Campbell. Again the return answer was, "he could not come." Peggy's answer to the second turn down was, "that's what the *man* says—God has said otherwise!" "Write him again! He will be here within two weeks!!" He was!

Andrew Woolsey, the biographer of Duncan Campbell, said he was still not willing to preach. Woolsey also said that Peggy had a Holy intimacy with the Lord. How right he was. She says she withstood Campbell just as Paul withstood Peter to his face. She had asked the preacher to come to a small, isolated village to hold a meeting. Duncan told Peggy she was wasting her time. The people of the village were not in favor of the revival type meetings he was known to produce. He also told her he doubted her wisdom in this thing. At that rebuke, Peggy turned in the direction of his voice, her sightless eyes seeming to penetrate his soul, and said,

"Mr. Campbell, sir, if you were living as near to God as you ought to be, He would reveal His secrets to you, also." Duncan accepted the rebuke. Then he knelt with Peggy and the dear intercessor prayed her heart, *"Lord, you remember what you told me this morning, that in this village you are going to save many souls but especially seven men who will be pillars in the church of my fathers. Lord, I have given your message to your servant, Mr. Campbell, and he seems not prepared to accept it. Oh Lord, give him wisdom, because he badly needs it."*

Duncan went to the village that night and preached on Acts 17:30: *"The times of ignorance God winked at; But now commands all men everywhere to repent."* As he was preaching, many in the congregation broke out in agonizing cries of great spiritual distress. Many were crying out to the Lord for the repentance of sins. By the time he was finished preaching, the entire congregation was mourning for their sins. Among them, Peggy's seven men. The Revival was on!

"Blessed are those who hunger and thirst for righteousness, for they shall be filled."

(MATTHEW 5:6)

CHAPTER EIGHT

SISTER QUAN

"There is a great host of preachers who have literally cast aside the message of the cross of Jesus Christ! It doesn't matter what anyone tells you about a great 'revival' or moving of the Spirit taking place; it doesn't matter how many multitudes are involved, or how loud their praises are; it doesn't matter how 'successful' a particular ministry may appear. If the cross of Jesus Christ is not the door through which people come, you can rest assured—it is not the work of God."

— DAVID WILKERSON

"Depend upon it, if you are bent on prayer, the devil will not leave you alone. He will molest you, tantalize you, block you, and will surely find some hindrances... I do not think he minds *our praying about things if we leave it at that. What he minds, and opposes steadily, is the prayer that prays on until it is prayed through, assured of the answer."*

— MARY WARBURTON BOOTH

"It is time to cry out, O Church of the Lord Jesus Christ! Put on the whole armor of God! Clothe yourself in the gifts of the Spirit! Go out against the enemy and destroy him! Bring to the Kingdom of God glory and majesty because He is the King of Kings and the Lord of Lords! You and I should see victories every day and never know defeat!"

— LESTER SUMRALL

How passionate is our walk with Jesus? How deep is our trust and how strong is our faith in our God? King David said:

"...Earnestly, will I seek you; my soul thirsts for You; my flesh longs for You..."

(PSALM 63:1)

"...As the deer pants for the water brooks, so my soul pants for You, Oh Lord."

(PSALM 42:1)

Jesus said we are to *"... love the Lord your God with* all *your heart,* all *your soul, with* all *your mind and with* all *your strength." (Mark 12:30)* Do we?

What do we really give all of our "all's" to? Is it to self-indulgence, our comfort, our jobs, our cars, our goals in life, our businesses, our family, our football teams, our retirement savings, our houses, our clothing? All these things are good but the Holy Spirit once told me, "Whatever monopolizes your mind the majority of the time, that is your God." In America, we are so blessed with prosperity that the blessings have become our snare. "Lest when you have eaten and are full, and have built beautiful houses and dwell in them... and your silver and gold are multiplied, and all that you have is multiplied; when your heart is lifted up and you forget the Lord your God... then you say in your heart, *"My power and the might of my hands have gained me this wealth." (Deuteronomy 8:12-17)*

Jesus told the rich young man, who lived a life worthy of reward, that he lacked one thing because his heart was full of the world (Mark 10:21).

I know you are thinking that I've gone from writing to preaching to meddling. Am I? Picture this. There you are, as usual, living, loving, laughing and being happy, totally engrossed with what is going on around you. You are consumed with the world, and all its trappings, enjoying all your fun, when a government official comes up and puts a gun to your head and says, *"Deny Christ or Die."* What would you do? (Selah)

It was 1983; Christians in China were being killed and persecuted daily. Thousands had their homes taken away from them; families were broken up and sent to slave labor camps. Pastors were brutalized. Many of these men of God had their ears, fingers, and toes cut off in front of their people. One was drowned in the urine of the congregation while they were made to watch. Church doors were kicked open and Christians were lined up around the walls, and one by one, with a gun to their heads, were asked to deny Christ or die. In a church of 275 worshipers in the Henan Province, only three chose to live.

This drove the Christians to meet secretly in houses. According to Dan Wooding, who reported on Sister Quan, she was a courageous house church leader from the Henan Province of China.

In September 1983, she was sentenced to life in prison for her Christian activities. However, after a harrowing imprisonment, she was eventually released and immediately returned to active leadership status in the house church.

In a secret interview with a ministry called Open Doors, Sister Quan relates her story:

> *"Quan is not her real name. In China, it is common for Christians who are speaking out to change their names for protection.*
>
> *"In 1983-1984, the Chinese government decided to 'clean up' the society of Christians. It was called the 'Anti-Spiritual Pollution Campaign.' At that time, evangelical Christianity was growing throughout the country. Henan Province was the hot bed. These Christians were very brave and bold in declaring the Gospel of Jesus. Great signs and wonders followed them wherever they went. According to the secret police, these activities*

became excessive. The government then started to arrest church leaders. Rounding up believers became a daily routine for the police. The law, that officials said was being broken, was 'idolatry' or 'mysticism/superstition,' since they did not understand Christianity.

"The Chinese officials told those they arrested that they were being held, 'because you have blind worship/superstition.' They were given a chance to give their allegiance to a state-sponsored church called the Three Patriotic Movement Church. Anyone who refused to join were taken before a court and either sent to prison or death."

The police arrested Sister Quan and her entire family: brothers, sisters, husband, in-laws, and older relatives. They took her son and daughter (ages one and four) and sent them off to become wards of the state. For over one month, they were questioned and tortured and forced to endure intense humiliation and persecution. The time finally came for sentencing. Since Sister Quan's entire family refused to recant the name of Jesus, her husband and mother in-law were executed by a firing squad in front of the family. Sister

Quan was given a life sentence. Her younger sister was sentenced to 15 years and her two brothers and other family members were sentenced to various prison terms.

Before they were sentenced, the government gave them all a chance to go free by just denying Jesus. They all refused. Once again, I ask the question, *"What would you do?"*

Sister Quan and her sister were sent to a women's hard labor prison camp. She said in the interview that life in the camp was extremely hard. There were days when they had to live and sleep in their own waste and filth. The guards would constantly use different methods to try to persuade her to deny her faith.

> *"She said, 'Through it all, I could feel God was with me. That was the only reason I could endure that place.'*
>
> *"Regular criminals were in the prison, also. Sister Quan and her sister would use every opportunity they could to preach to them. Many came to the knowledge of salvation. The more pressure put on the new Christians to deny their faith, the more the gospel in the prison*

increased-instead of decreasing. Every day more souls were saved for the Kingdom of God.

"The prison officials then set up an anti-Christian system. For non-Christians, the system set up a chance for sentence reduction for good behavior. This was not available for Christians.

"Sister Quan said, 'If they would only say, 'I don't believe,' they would get one year sentence reduction. They didn't even have to say they didn't believe in Jesus. Praise God, even the new Christians had the strength from the Lord not to say this.'"

Sister Quan stated that she didn't have a Bible with her in prison, and the visitors (one day a month) could not easily pass one because the prison guard was right there the whole time. They had to pass it fast and hide it while the guard went to the toilet.

"A few times a week, the guards would search the entire area of where the prisoner's cell is and if something is found, the prisoner is punished," said the Open Door worker. *"They had to find*

creative ways to hide the Bible. They don't know when the search will be.

"Some were assigned to a prison house with twenty per house and they normally didn't do body searches—but then, when they found out that a Christian had Bibles, they sometimes did body searches and found books, so some got half a month in solitary confinement because of this. From that time on, they didn't carry the Bible in their clothing. If they were caught reading the Bible, it would be confiscated, so they had to wake up at one or two in the morning and secretly try to read under the blanket."

At this point in the interview, Sister Quan actually smiled and laughed as she recalled the ways they used to hide the Bibles. *"We would break the Bible into parts and one brother would keep one part and one sister kept another, so at least if it's discovered, they would still have some,"* she said.

The Lord rewarded her faithfulness. It wasn't long before the fire of the Holy Ghost descended on the prison. This institution had about five hundred people held there. More than four hundred came to know the Lord. Some prisoners, who were so sick that they couldn't work, were brought to the prison hospital, and for some of them the doctors said there was no hope. Sister Quan and other Christians would then go into the room and pray for the sick and they would be healed, to the shock of the doctors. Consequently, even many of the prison officials came to the Lord.

After some time and much prayer, Sister Quan's sentence was reduced to a specific number of years, instead of life. Finally, after 13½ years, she was released on July 1996. God had given her strength to bring revival to the most unlikely place.

Throughout all those years, she prayed fervently for her son and daughter who were taken away from her. She pleaded with the Lord that they were not brought up as puppets of the Chinese government. God answered her faithfulness with the desires of her heart. After five months of searching, she discovered both of them. They were members of an underground Pentecostal Christian Church. Her daughter was now age 17 and her son, 14. Her daughter was leaving school early so she could go and preach the Gospel full time.

Sister Quan was a leader before she was arrested and is a church leader again now that she is free. Friends constantly warn her to lay low but she says it doesn't matter—she's used to prison anyway. She believes that nothing worse could happen to her than what she has already experienced. She often quotes: *"For I consider that the sufferings of the present time are not worthy to be compared with the glory which shall be rewarded in us."* (Romans 8:18:)

Amen.

"… we ourselves, boast of you among the churches of God for your patience and faith in all persecutions and tribulation that you endure: Which is manifest evidence of the righteous judgment of God, that you may be counted worthy of the Kingdom of God, for which you also suffer."

(2 THESSALONIANS 1:4-5)

ABOUT THE AUTHOR

Frank "J. J." Di Pietro, before becoming an independent researcher and author, spent several decades in radio broadcasting. Di Pietro is widely recognized for his devoted prayer life and zeal for revival. DiPietro, and his wife Melissa, moved to Kansas City to be near family and be a part of a global revival movement.

You can reach Di Pietro on his Facebook author page:
https://www.facebook.com/frankjjdipietro

Fiind out more about his books at:
TheResurgenceStore.com

Also Available From Christos Publishing:

CARRIERS OF THE FIRE
VOLUMES 1-5

Each of these volumes feature the stories of devout, Spirit-led Christians from previous generations. The tales of old often enable us to experience a move of God afresh.

Fiind out more at TheResurgenceStore.com

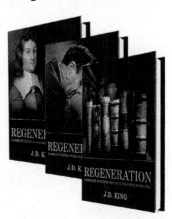

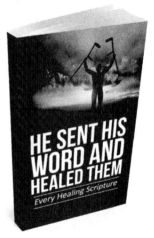

Also Available From Christos Publishing:

Why You've Been Duped Into Believing That The World Is Getting Worse

"For us Baby Boomer Christians who grew up on The Late Great Planet Earth, the future was deliciously and fascinatingly evil. J.D. King, in his latest book, asserts that we have been "duped" by this gloomy view of the future. Via numerous documented metrics, King shows that the influence of Christian values—and the growth of Christianity itself—is raising the quality of life around the globe."

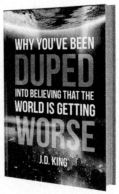

—**JON MARK RUTHVEN, PhD.**
Author of *On the Cessation of the Charismata* and *What's Wrong with Protestant Theology*

Find out more at TheResurgenceStore.com

Christos
Publishing

Also Available From Christos Publishing:

SHIFT
LEADING IN TRADITION

"This short primer offers fresh wisdom for the biggest need of the hour—solid, godly leaders who can bring sustainable change to the world around them."

-Brad Herman
Harrison House

Find out more at TheResurgenceStore.com

Printed in Great Britain
by Amazon

81166112R00078